GW01150931

West Of Yesterday

– Stride –

By the same author:
The Sleep Switch (Odyssey)
Ode To A Bic Biro, After Wittgenstein (Trombone Press)
Binary Myths: conversations with contemporary poets
[editor] (A Stride Conversation Piece)
Vital Movement [contributor] (Reality Street 4 Packs)

WEST OF YESTERDAY
Andy Brown

WEST OF YESTERDAY
First edition 1998
© Andy Brown
All rights reserved
ISBN 1900152 31 2

Cover photo © Andy Brown
Cover design by Neil Annat

Acknowledgements
*Angel Exhaust, Brink, Exeter Poetry Prize Anthology, Fire,
Journal of Contemporary Anglo-Scandinavian Poetry,
New Hope International Poetry Forum, Oasis, Odyssey,
Poetry: A Blueprint For Key Stage 3* (Stanley Thornes Pub. Ltd.),
*Poetry & Audience, Psychopoetica, Rustic Rub, Terrible Work,
Trembling Ladders* (Australia)

'Fifth force guru', '& when she sang' and 'In time'
were used as lyrics on the XC-NN album *Lifted*

Published by
Stride Publications
11 Sylvan Road, Exeter
Devon EX4 6EW

with assistance from
the Ralph Lewis Award
at the University of Sussex

Contents

& it snows

The lute girl's lament 10
This meeting in each other 11
Villaneuva 12
Talking about your face 13
Happens all the time 14
Domestic vignette 15
Adverse weather 16
Journey of the Duendes 17
Going on 18
How it ends 19
As it always was 20
Blue irises 21
& it snows 22

Some improvements

Some improvements 24
All intervening yesterdays 28
Tibetan uplift 32
Summa 35
Impermanently yours 38
Excavating morning 40
Between us 42
Exodus 43
Lux 44

Coastal service

In this house, on this morning 46
Quote it's a man's world unquote 48
What is poetry? 49
Coastal service 50
Sleeping on it 51
Agreeing with them 52
Migrating south 53
In time 54
Language of the dying body 55
It's done with mirrors 56
Down tube 57

Exurbia *58*
Fifth force guru *59*
Pictures of everyday life *60*
Two specks crossing the ice *61*
Blowing out the candles *62*
Libra *63*
Smorgasbord *64*
Into the turbulent light *65*
Tufts of grass *66*
Autumn drama *67*
The night café *68*
& when she sang *69*
A moment *70*
From ideas to things *71*
The tortoise pokes its head
clean through the bangle *72*

for Amy

& it snows

The lute girl's lament
(after Po Chu-Yi)

By night & by the riverside goodbyes were spoken
but no guitar   no flute was heard.
Words of cold farewell beneath the bright
moon above the body of the stream.

Beneath the maples' flower-like leaves
the river branched & where the maples ended
the river began a new world of level country
stilled by the grip of frost.

In the exact moment when
the rest was silence
Host forgot to leave   Guest lingered on
but no guitar or flute was heard.

'& so I laughed myself from year to year
& the red skirts of song were stained with wine

but like the torrent the music was lulled

& dark greeted the paling constellations.'

This meeting in each other

They make an 'ideal couple' & the orchids he keeps sending
constitute a cross-section of fact –
a river searching into sleep again.
Night comforts the day
the other seems perfect
& that's why the lips move
the intricate tactile language.
Notice their mouth-to-mouth greeting
talking with chemicals
the yellow marble showing signs of heat
the nose set at the heart & night
by mirror light that turns the faces into masks

& the dark held out the dead man's arm
his hand a little thing of wax
her own hand an exquisite peach marquee
& she brought him the snowstorm
to bathe in the lake
to wash his mouth & hands
& when his mouth was cleansed
she followed the dead man weeping night
her tears like ants uncountable
& sleeper driven on she
rose near morning
the skyline & a distant choosing
between the creaking angles of surprise.

Villaneuva

Immediately one is tempted & it's over
imagining parallels with higher creatures
like man.   This selective distortion of reality
is even more true of still photos
the same thing   this   that was beginning
with next when what we have runs out.

They thought about that one for weeks   unable
to imagine anything as static & passive as towels
marked His & Hers could be causing the problem
but they let us know no answer is possible
only experience   & that's okay   so much of it
evaporates before the sea   the best we can do is
leave it alone   bubbling like Club Soda.
'Let's go to Joni's bar & pick up a couple of bottles.'

Talking about your face

He doesn't want to know there's music
but there is sometimes
a river in the mountains
in with the serious stuff
beyond Yes & No.

Yet to wedge it all into the middle
of the night   somewhere near Dublin
matters on some kind of level.   There
they were   looking right at it
in a moment that adds up with rain.

It had to happen.   Everything that happened
was there – the nervous system
the number that tells the time –
resolving itself in counterpoint to acts.

Happens all the time

His mind was a picture of home
each time he witnessed himself
return.   It made him laugh
'myself that this was'
memories trickling
down from the sky like   ramp

& so he stood there with his head
containing its own outcomes
the ones on his wrists
two comfy chairs
turning another page
infesting the idea of himself.

It's not that he doesn't know why
but here he is   starting up the car.

Domestic vignette

He painted her in animate words.
Naturally life became burdensome.
The glans was plainly audible
asking for a rest.   He bit the dusk.

Wherever he stayed he left footprints
carefully wrapped in wax paper.
The hours   the days   perhaps the years
extinguished the candle & couple.

She wrung her hand guns till they sweated
moulding an ear around his void
nude as they were in their faces.

'I love you'   gets said
most often when lying
like this   side by side.

Adverse weather

The time drew close
sketching on the edge of the sofa
illuminated by some thought or other
that slunk off into a corner.

The words meditated.
Truth smiled in silence.
As sunrise contemplated the window
two shadows tumbled down the stairs.

Morning did nothing
nailed fast in that position
as if life could keep working forever.
The blinds stayed firmly closed.

Journey of the Duendes

Not a day goes by   then laughter
peals across the lake   especially
on the nights when hailstones break
the windows.   The faces on the other bank
don't understand distance   only time
'one day's travel & worth a look'   they say.

From the heights the pentatonic floated –
probably attempts at self-diagnosis –
& the skinny-legged flautists began to dance
friendlier   wiser   & not so frustrating.   You cried
a red salt lake six miles in length with islands.
I sent a boat out to an island   moored & sank
up to my lips.   Few roads & no bridges exist.

It became routine to be saving each other's lives.

Going on

Go on.　You can.
I am the end of
what is always
rupture.

'Love me' – not the
distrusted form of
me　&　from
understanding　go on.

How it ends

About what we did   nothing
yet still we persist in living it
like a sudden burst of   raison d'être.
In that briefest of moments   the noise
of the underground river rose
a night full of red   & we should have been happy
'it's all make-believe   we forget that sometimes.'

Those flowers didn't smell much
but neither did distasteful things
left trapped in the light – words like *betrayal*
& *garden*   starting to get dark –
surprised by the formulas that come to mind.
Were we ready to live without them?
Well… but that was enough for now.

As it always was

Moving deeper through the waves
the intense blue April sky suits
the moment as if choreographed.

The mists of pre-history begin to lift
& the possibility develops that here
pressed in between the universal appeal

of the meaning of life
we're gathered in mirror
awaiting each other again.

Blue irises

Existence over   other days will be
transported to the cliff
I am trying to scale   your face
the one you are wearing.

Here & there the ground beneath our feet
yet miniature oases bloom
the interminable banquet of things
meniscus of a bubble.

& it snows

Thermometer marks barely
a notch above freezing
the air is harsh & piercing –

& hazards an alternative   the shoulders
circle into cocoon & carpet
the chance show in tireless,
distilling the flow of the sleeper.
Observers crowd into the cyclone
& malt a soundtrack evocative of time.
Its warren is brutal & duplicates;
the dull nooks
shrink her tones & drowse in purr.

It's not only hatred she detests:
urinals   stalwart topicalists
these also alter her attested state
with fists that squeeze like insomnia
taking her beyond the poplars
puzzle to Aurora Borealis.
The snow from sill with shovel
certifies   the void that's known
is small next to the void
the particles of the air bequeath –

against the white.
I am colourblind   but fingerprint
the word *celadon*   to celebrate
its willow green prizes.

Some improvements

Some improvements

1.

Moving from snapshot to motion picture
a moment sees someone guard their time.
The desire to land is understandable...
years have gates through which the blurred
edges & open shapes of living things
adapt to the process of healing
from the moment
they get up in the morning
until the moment
they get up in the morning
writing out the details of anxious silence
with ritual annotations
& imitations that steal the day
receiving our shuffles & cries.

Living there & lying awake   the answers
sleep & the city collapses
meaning   the miracle of outer surfaces
is crushed even more powerfully.
Afterwards it disappears & this is
the force that turns it into the mystery
one thousand or more books locked up.

We follow the silent chapters & translate
the main qualities of the emotion into a name –
the prologue to possessing an unalterable shape.
A temporary animal might recognise the difference
with dreamy detachment   merely
by shape & arrangement
& alone succeed where home habits
let us relentlessly examine
a piece of wo-
a fragment of a word
& we shall see it all again later
life upon life
as these apparent tracks lead us back to the main road.

2.

It was chiefly a matter of feeling.
Friends filled with the ease of
forgetfulness   rotated noises in their ears.
But the languor & softness of the blood
was a kind of sleep
safely delivering opinions to the world
with the sterile stroke that comes from
the daily routine of nerve centres in the brain.

Nostalgia is ruined when we think.
The idea of going back fades
an undesirable dream
but measures the changes over our lives
& what did we care so long as we got better?
Years are the brief oblivion   the secret
incendiarism that living ferments.
In our own time we need the stimulus of what is past
but are more interested in our own headaches
with an adult's fascination for toys
as if warm blood bestowed immortality.
We lie at the water's edge
awaiting our turn on the pyre
while old men dispense folk medicine
solving the problems with nicknames
& the little things we learn.
The problem is straightforward –
we are all others
& cannot even distinguish *yes* from *no* .

Eventually   they say   a miracle occurs –
the doors reopen & the new road
winds back to the old city.
People said trees wouldn't grow here
but look   blossom!
& it was true
as far as we could see
the crude walls were covered at last
in blooms of avalanche.

3.

Needs catch at what is
living & growing.
Proliferating tissues
fill the imagination.

The past seems safer
because of the oblivion
that overtakes – the unseen
but prophesied abyss.

Life we can easily imagine.
Personality leaps before our eyes
& after its creator's death

fatality seems to hang
plunging its hands   calmly
into a swarm of bees.

4.

Words alone are the last echo
from the chaos of the beginning.
Parades of people who are sentenced
punctuate along their unending progression.
Some walk patiently in circles
others sprawl in knots of laughter
(things modern people wear)
the floodlit public   hopelessly divided
masks over mouths & noses
in case we accidentally breathe

& although in theory the complex system might leak
we go round & round the closed circuit like the previous day
taking extraordinary forms.
Sometimes life is only visible
after we have gone –
like certain insects
& hermaphrodite gods
it propagates itself
all by itself
in its own image.

All intervening yesterdays

1.

Critical light
in typical scene
a certain smile
& then the eyes
you cannot miss
but sit across
& then you notice
in the sky
a kind of gesture
two by two
the eyes half-open
softer edges
fontanelle not
fully shut
in touch
& makes you fireworks.

Delivered on
the wind
this love
that falls
as yellow rain
chaotic now
monsoon of abstract
wave erosion
west of London
in min
i
mal
energy
in a man
ner of
speaking
reliving each mile
the air you breathe
into my face
just think
we're only kids

& we can do it
in the sea
our minds
in the sea

but we don't have to
wait that long
at extreme elevations
'when the sun swims under the earth'
as the Incas put it —

our time
releases
anodynes
frozen in
misshapen stones
emotional river gorge

& we fanned out to search for each other.

2.
When night overtakes
nude to the sky
chip away the parts
that aren't element.

What has gone into it?
No matter
how many things
go on
is it worth being
if I can't do this?

Faces have numbers.
You can live in them
& get around.

3.
& my boat drifted toward the mainland.
A hill.
I waved.
For less I'd go back
& I wanted to ladder
the morning sky
a blue balloon
that drops away
into the sea
each second of night
strained through
your breaths
tighter than pipes
motionless
& waited for the earth's
rotational
axis.
It was a simple accident.

4.
We looked like babies
in winter   last winter
& found ourselves
in narrow streets
till late in the day
& we passed once more
through the loop
of each other
in tiny cloud
between our lips
remoulded from past
occupations.

& when your breath
hit my face

morning sun flooded the Kazakhstan steppes.

5.
It was midnight –
it would not spoil.
It was possible –
no one had done it before.
Much of the area
remained unmapped –
the river after all
makes the rules
& some lines of evidence
suggest it helps
to forget how we
ourselves behave
ceremonial or not,

but it takes an atom of oxygen
2000 years
to complete the cycle
& whilst I am waiting
for your breath to return
in simple measures
by all of this & more,
decay & eruptions
that give it a name
change its form
from a home on the coast
to a house on a hill.

Naked
scarps
the wind
wakes up.
We have
showers & smile
a lot
at one
another.

Tibetan uplift

Blank spaces
on time maps

a maze
without plans

springing from ante
cedent courses

Irrawaddy &
Mekong   a

bathed & hymned
Tibetan uplift

devotional circum
ambulation

isthmus   'navel
of the earth'

the matted
lotus pericarp

mens' skulls for
drinking

drums &
thighbones

rescued & secure.
Yab & Yum united –

circle   water
square   earth –

forcing their minds
along its banks

learning into
what is meant

by re turn –
an error of juggling.

•

Upper courses
fountain head

the Brahmaputra of Assam
the Tsangpo of Tibet.

The water now forces
a cavernous passage

& precipitates
culture & myth –

the cavern the form
of a formless head

intercut
by deep response

with a theodolite
as when anonymous

presses a daub
adobe abodes

tall deodars
& flowering rhododendrons.

•

Independent freebooter
on language's high seas

sites the invisible
sources by tunnel

attempting itself
in water hearsay.

The sources lie
beyond the writing

surrounded by these
pencilled comments

in the margin
above us & elsewhere –

a journey as possible
number of steps

carrying your own load
& the loads of others as well.

Summa

Insomnia skewered
they wanted to float
a cathode ray blinking –
exhilarating work
on the baby (died when born.)

A mouth was sitting propped up
X required
not a word be said.
A word stood by –
the wasted idea of a century.

•

To kill time there were doctors
whose religion lay
discredited
priests without organ
transplants   turning

the face-bearing clouds
of vapour into
little blobs of life –
this sensation   the injection
& the weeks of waiting.

•

The label that said *Mirror*
yesterday   still says it today
so once you are buried   relax.
As when hot slabs of cake
melt the icing

the whole masterpiece is slippery.
You cannot dig yourself out
& you're in too deep for friends to find.
After 3 hours of burial
the soft & yielding clouds hang low

they are now what they are
what they are now what are they?
heat from the meteorite?
men in a spilled graveyard?
I want you to read my funeral oration.

•

To avoid the summit
there against the void
the little angel went out hunting
a slim volume of drivel.
Everyone went off to the countryside

suffering some essential point
in the middle of emotion
to call on existing immortals.
Summer meanwhile let its surface
split open near the front

unearthing sweet meanings;
handling the petals in such a way
we could literally forget
the Bible has been studied in this fashion –
the threshold of faith & atheism.

•

The world was sorted into groups –
alive / not alive
she   is another category
the gospel of nothing in the world
& the institution of private property

arranged in a shallow box –
flat & thin irregular pieces
sitting in the darkness with the scientist's
life's works – deep accounts of notions infinite
being & no   thingness   kept in self defence & ceramic jars.

•

All day   night came
shadowed in bone
& there you stood   there
with your head   sometimes
reaching the ceiling & even beyond the ceiling

yourself except for
the supporting framework
of timbers & speech to match the walls.
To be   is to keep quiet & watch for developments.
Nothing to do to it now but try it – people in the present tense:

'Shall I not go on?'
'No. Not now. Go away.'
'Has anything happened?'
'If I need you I'll call.'
Go & read the Apocalypse in a world where numbers don't exist.

Impermanently yours

resurrection like
direction / nightmare
or is it vice-versa?
probably   probably not
extending out over the
water   flexible membrane
in after image colour glow
on Congo   Ob   the Yellow River
where the fire is
putting out to meet
the pygmy chief
had not yet met
another on earth
the head   the hairdo
this was steel
on the level of pedestal
tube   & swing it
the sun   white bone
beneath a pinkish
pony of beer
monkey to a laughing world
balloon trying to rise
an inch above the eyes
broadleaf brain
a plume of almost
forgot about the
bright noon turning
from blue to grey
deodorized
in mouth   speech finished
a tongue that knew
philosophy
machete sweating
me who he was
face in basin
in the depression & crowd
name of the little nation
hutmates
this is a democracy

running out of body
muscular / mental
hydrogen images
picked up in the light
of an explosion
the time between
the click & boom
locates the star
in area of 3
an improvised version
invented numbers
plastic lines
emotional cattle
olfactory backing
an ingress of freight
where tourists could see many.

In principle the practice
gave a rose in reply
scores of red
cylindrical body
shadows of the outflung
& the universe bumped
against a second
nettled   as measured
by sonar   toggle
on the instrument
closed circuit TV podium
bonanza of the aftermath
through smoke white birds
evaporated
water   (this puddle you tested)

forces change them
in time   as possible
word for identity –
beau ti ful –
have been spared.

Excavating morning

Gently inhale the tiny paper
(black smudge on your cheek)
an unresolved dependency.

•

I should dig each morning
thin layers of words arranged in time.
(I should avoid strenuous exercise throughout the summer months because
    of hazardous air pollution.)

•

The desert waits – sun-blush   mesa –
map page 31 to 2
the numbers growing.

•

Differences in the ratio of light
serrated like a steak knife
like a peacock's tail.

•

Problems don't begin & end with aardvark
but march right on through the alphabet –
a mirror of entertainment.

•

I was thinking instead of what hadn't been seen –
spillage on the listening rocks, pulse of the sun-bleached concrete –
something else that drew us in.

•

Before long the idea institutes the concept of institutions –
city skylines, cryptobiotic soil
a ripple in the experience.

•

Here in the shade of a morning as I mosey through infrastructure
a dark coloured crust covers most of the written world –
a time meniscus steeped in the life-affirming stink promise erodes.

•

Rest in your understanding. Avoid unmarked shallows.
Vibrate the clear blue sky passing the bluff.
Auto-pilot fluxgate compass.

Between us

Bored with sleeping
we carry chance
a 3-note chant
he-hah he-hoh
a method I
can't understand
no written language
stored by signals
the mail runner
notes from friends
on gramophone &
magic lantern
computer visor
tactile gloves
white envelopes
black edged
projected
'don't worry if you
read in papers'
published version
optimism
met & talked on
casual basis
chested voice
the unknown tract
relaxed if not
entirely friendly
'hello is Olwen there?'
sorry   wrong number
a kind of mapping
amused themselves
in speculation
were endless.

Exodus

System lies in key to
measure   tempting gaps
their satisfactions
explorations of the
landslide   bare & tinted
satellite photos
compact bodies
a cute sense & habit
nothing   just alive
but still possessing
chits for percolation
seepage
a virtual monotony
of talismans in deeper
purple of the mass
alternate bands of
white & lunar botanist
hot weather leaves
no date or distance
vector   time
& so the reader
's completely lost
no!   the faintest
mnemonic detail
thought by chanting
soubriquets
or by reversing letters of
your name   enjambement
rose explorer
known simply as
language   boiling water
beads on the rosary
flowing in &
out of it.

Lux
(for Rupert Loydell)

The state of being
active or functioning.
Emergence of an infant or young from the body of its mother.
Reflection of sound waves from a scream.
Still lives.
Self-portraits.
Slices fulfilling desire.

Paintings or drawings of inanimate objects such as bottles or flowers.
The scope of history with the fruits of the trees of the genus *Malus*.
Air in more or less rapid natural motion after the condensed moisture of the atmosphere
falls visibly in separate drops.
Riot in the solidity of fog.
Pictures of objects representing words.
Still lives.
Landscapes.
An effect produced in notion or belief.

White lines & several circles between light.
Memories of minutiae.
The twinge of belongings
like scar tissue
like initial creation.
A basket of fruit.
Newton's apple.
The overwhelming thud that signals something very *this*.

Coastal service

In this house, on this morning

A plane will glide more easily if rubbed with a candle –
remember to relight the pilot.   Light bulbs
last longer & give off more light if you strain them
through old stockings.   Use nylons to store opinions.
During a power cut the same rules apply: electricity & water
make a recipe – use it as a jigsaw puzzle.

An electric lightbulb makes a good mushroom.
Bread can be used to remove light stains.
Dab luminous paint on light switches.   Remember
if the head is allowed to dry out completely
when not in use it will crack & break up –
take it off & unplug the holes with a darning needle.

When hanging a long day   nap in the right direction,
run a bar of soap along the wrong side & monitor its progress
as you pull it through.   Try not to interrupt your work
if you're painting ceilings, walls or floors
as this will tend to make them perish.   Use a whisk
to save time.   Save time by keeping near the phone.

As your children grow older they are easier to let down.
Prevent this by putting a ball of cotton wool in the end of each finger.
Write letters & seal them with a little egg white.
Always iron the paper & avoid going in a straight line.
Stagger the line while greasing spots on separate sheets.
Wipe the line clean & free of water droplets.

Put a piece of white paper under each foot.   Smooth
some French chalk or talcum over the area before you start
then rub a little paraffin inside your shoes to smarten up
a limp lettuce.   If all else fails   scour a blocked drain
in this manner: make an X incision in the stem
& check for cracks in folding leaves.   Float in the cistern.

Fold in air bubbles for a fluffier poem.   Restore a dented
ping pong ball.   To make an inconspicuous join
sew decorative patches over worn out places & feelings –
it is easier with an odd number than an even.
International symbols in pattern books make excellent
wastepaper baskets;   chilli sauce an unusual cat repellent.

Use manners as a small vice. Slip your hands into plastic
sandwich bags.   If you can't change the water every day
use a pastry brush to remove fluff from working parts.   If you can,
use eyebrow tweezers to pull out stray pieces – you will find it
easier to extract what you want.   Put the stone back
into the avocado & seal.   & lastly, the skirting.

Quote it's a man's world unquote

it's a man's world
it's a manacle world
it's a manager world
it's a manageable world
it's a mandala world
it's a mandatory world
it's a mannequin world
it's a manicure world
it's a mange world
it's a mangle world
it's a mania world
it's a manual world
it's a manifest world
it's a manifesto world
it's a manifold world
it's a manky world
it's a manipulate world
it's a manna world
it's a mannerism world
it's a manouevre world
it's a manslaughter world
it's a mañana world
it's a manuscript world
it's a mantra world
it's a mantrap world
it's a manure world
it's a manner of world

What is poetry?

Thing.

A song.

A sixth sense.

A puppet.

Rather wry.

Foreign.

Trendy.

Black words.

Naked in the mind.

What the poem is.

Open.

The words begin tearing.

Isn't it attentiveness?

Sex before aching.

Coastal service

O kiosk! yr bright paint
chips   with beans   on poems
'stop off & eat'   you call
decaying softly.

O cashier! snatching secret
snacks   behind yr text
on post-structuralism
you give too much change

but Adam always gives it back
discussing ethics   the only fruit
those of us who've lost our teeth
can still eat comfortably   like ice-cream.

O knickerbocker glory!   yr presence
remains a model for theories
of left-field art –
you have soaked the sunny side up.

O sunbathing Eve!   the red head of
twilight deconstructs the shadows
of a distant flavour – come in
for Adam's found the kiosk.

O kiosk!
O cashier!
O knickerbocker glory!
O Adam!   O Eve!

Sleeping on it

It's really not an ugly town
but let's go back
inside your dream
the candle stumps
& pictures seen at home.

Our lives have already taken place
surrounded by useless moments
which cannot be the very same thing
as life in drag
or could that be tenderness?

Yet early   very early
when the lilac coloured voice & choir
dies away into the distance
fragile as a dandelion's seed puff

as if at by unspoken chance
the man from Cohen's corner store
creamy-white in a grey-blue void
knows that something's happened –

'My life at last has
meaning / measles / mealtime / meat / meadow'

Agreeing with them

It proves to be a compelling idea
the backdrop to living
& somehow they begin to search for hidden objects
like sound flowing through an hourglass.
Of course there is a fifty-fifty chance
of taking that road randomly
so if Colin is dead & Colin is alive
there simply must be two of them.   Rats
don't work things out this way
struggling with the fork
in the ongoing road of real life.

But the children   & ostensibly the panda
give the powerful impression
the empty garage somehow is salient for them
the world is a film run slowly elsewhere
making the mountains task abstract
& the notion of a point of view inapt
for this is not an error they are likely to make. . .

'Zoubab cut off her daddy's head
but she has got some very strong glue.'

Migrating south

If I were you I wouldn't start from here
across the velvet ribbon river
things are more lively

---

perhaps the first thing to remember is
that air's elastic
& so we can play tunes on it
dawn chorus.

You will see from the aerial photograph

. this line is being used as middle C.

In time

The tellers of creation myths have short
memories   *laying out a slalom course /
feeling claustrophobic about time.

In a room of deliberately forgotten things
the windows are dark glasses   sliding
down our faces like tectonic plates.

Tunnels branch out from them
though only one reaches
daylight – the entrance on level ten.

Our guide won't go deeper.   He believes
the devil hangs out on nine
giving motivational lectures
to corporate executives.

(*Delete)

Language of the dying body

Earth made them
lay aside work –
a hospital manual
'How not to be afraid of death'.

Such is the strength of a dog's soul!
melange mongrel
Spooner's vendeuse doing what
pond life produces   a democratic language
'rhubarb rhubarb rhubarb'
psittacoid cognomas   'who's a pretty boy then?'
bluff sweat & tease
phrases that are what we think,
but I don't think that what I think *is* anymore.
Thought as mediating ideas & vice-versa.

It's done with mirrors

so if the burden of memory is removed
the water bends the light.
Admit for once the Indian is right
even if he isn't
a shot of penicillin
inside your father's testicles.
It all depends on which
TV
channels you watch in the evenings
blended with the yellow melons
redolent of opium
& all the species of herbivorous hymenoptera.

Still   others cement these islands to the riverbanks of guts
accumulating identities or going out to encounter reality again
engaged in conversations which consist of silence.
In these as in others   easy   what was hard was to be
put down in the middle of nowhere
two perfect sized earthenware teapots
without a house in sight.   'You could get bored'
I thought   but I was wrong
because there is that
slightly out-of-focus past peeling from the walls
wherever you are   or is it that if you lift the branches
the nearness of an implacable ending starts
rising through the dynamics that surround us?

Something like that no doubt.   After we have accepted
these gifts   only symbols or ideas could be less perfect
learning that there is no this   there is no that
& it all happens without anyone knowing it
aroused by such a silence.

Down tube

& we understood everything – oops sorry –
but that's only the state story.
A change was needed   whereas
what we saw was a swing.

Meanwhile   over there   a short way off
the outlines of ideas were taking shape
saying something useful like 'un-huh'
pretending to be themselves to stretch
the words & fit them neatly into life
sucking at them & throwing away the skins.

What had we done to deserve television
like that?   The books sat in front of the screen
combing the politics out of their hair.

Exurbia

He ran off somewhere to the side
& that's how November began   narcotic
pushing out of the lower strata
in the direction of the bedroom.

Inside them at that moment spread
London   carpeted with oriental rugs.
Then droning far inland in tighter
spirals   6.6 sextillion tons

fatal to those with allergic reactions.
Skittish neutrals this that year
they were defector from America
collage   sculpture   tulips in a vase

a crowd with the family   handgun.
But what if the multi-million dollar solution
& experiments with rats & mice don't work?
'One by one the police take out the...'

It all takes place by night & by day
people simply forget about the explosions
blown away in clouds of dust & heavy doses
of political news.   Over.   Out.   Slow fade.

Fifth force guru

Though we cannot see most of them   even by daylight
by night the mind has frozen hard enough to walk across.
Birds flew   real life was lived   but a black slate roof
in what looked like twilight   who were we
to place an impossible dignity on things
clutching at pillows & muttering about mortality?

Watching a man lug his own weight I agreed
'you know you always cut up when you lose'
shreds of memory jumping from your head over to mine
in rituals combed forward to cover the baldness.

Sometimes simply breathing enough of it
to stay alive is trying   & the katabatic winds
arrange the jewels into dozens of unlabelled piles.
The mirrors rub their eyes in a life of reflexive reclusion.

Pictures of everyday life

What cumulative effect
the kind it is impossible to flee?
& yet we shuffle constantly
changing form from day to day
more concerned with soup
than the porridge that surrounds us –

the entire troposphere of habit
worshipped by the back door
before it is completely
out of the birth canal.
What is there to do;
remove yourself to a remote island?

I no longer make those
imaginary trips across London.

Two specks crossing the ice

Again the negotiations
crumble on contact with air.
The skinless sky reflects upon
the vast network.

A mass of factors present themselves
as close dark silhouettes
the faint suggestion of shifting profiles
liquefied by summer rains.

'To penetrate further we must have more powerful tools'
but the wind sweeps in & expands the hole
as if it has been opened from the wrist
carving parabolas in a version of life.

Whatever is out there   people rarely use the river.
They don't even like to sleep close to it.

Blowing out the candles

Talent.   They died at the water's edge
perhaps by a form of imprinting.
That & only that is what they were.

The artist led us across a grassy
bluff   the green depression
that had been the family

home.   Life for the most part
lay in an amorphous pile
applying bright layers of

pain.   Down in the valley
nirvanic man
abandoned the village & fled.

Libra

From the start inevitable
but what does it do when it gets there
floating down out of the endless
pale stratosphere into   meathook?

It all takes place while you are thinking
it   meaning   the paper windows
exist to help you clarify the themes
exempli gratia   a broken spout.

This to him is what makes it
real.   It explains his dreams.

Smorgasbord

Blossom tufts of forest keep the tourists restless.
They haven't had practice laughing at themselves.
But they *have* had their buffet & crossroad shrines.

Camping on a crowded beach two experts
throw a bomb into the water
as if by butcher knife.   Here too

the beach reveals a stagnant centre.
Only people with a living
memory wave goodbye.

Suddenly   applause behind us warm & steady
the mass demonstration & rumble of tanks.
I cannot say that we have seen the end of it

Into the turbulent light

To us they were the earliest perceptions
but we had to paddle hard the last few
miles   unsure of the new rules.

In the frame of the possible
the riverbanks looked tentative & people
too small for the buildings   the sky

in its place   lazing on the surface
creating sensations of weightlessness –
the type of truth that electrifies a crowd.

Gradually the head grows used to its own
weight on the pillow & we pass by like thumbnails
slowly drawn across the teeth of combs.

Tufts of grass

The problems?　it helps
if you rub them together
but the frequent showers
everybody loves to take
load trash & waste
into the process.

He clutches at such
tufts of grass
in order to avoid the city
& make headway in a poem
forgetting that this city is
in a poem – intense scent
of sunlit buildings –
depending on the distance.

Autumn drama

The fruits had ripened & would fall
one of them having cracks in it.
But that was not the only thing we thought –
all sorts of rubbish came to mind.

We walked along the bridge in volume
& there on the pavement perched
Nirvana.   The damaged bridge fell
to thinking about the cracks.

Having become mental cracks
they came full circus
but weren't what mattered.
What mattered instead

was the breach opening up in the rosy
pushing through the cracks between our lips.

The night café
(after Van Gogh)

On the right as you enter
on the edge of a thing complete
something to do with the white spaces
in between   something that amuses them.

We do the whole thing with paper
with an interest in painting   the worn out rugs
& that is why you're here   you came
without asking   the body one hundred percent.

Now is not impossible.   The notes
that attempt to explain it concisely
separate the darkness.   Retail prayer.
Eating the medium still remains an act of faith.

& when she sang

she fell from the tree & rose
in bubbling puddles
bound as she was to
the oceanic system.

Corridors of flowers
lined the sheets
teased up through
the waves & set on fire.

You could be sure
she would return
pulling back the walls
of the new religious lifestyle.

She fell & she flew with the light
out of the childhood & into the mist.

A moment

A self
>> portrait tattooed
> on the eyelids'
insides

is just as it is
>> not me or mine
> it is not self
true image   eye.

It thinks
>> there's thought
> in thinking
your future's

the shadow
>> of the present
> shining
on the past.

Illumination
>> the basic vision
> lying in the light
it throws.

From ideas to things

(Children talking about triangles:
'A triangle doesn't have a side on top.'
'If you had lots of triangles, you'd have
a lot of secret places for everyone.')

We
conceive
a triangle.

The definition of
a triangle is what it is.
We know what it is / is not –

heat
(in the
absence of cold)

cold
(in the
absence of heat) –

words
finding themselves
close upon the object.

The tortoise pokes its head clean through the bangle

The world unfolds
on map page two
as when an eye seems
to bend in the water.

It fits into our pockets
but there is no chance
only our ignorance
of slow uncomfy bus rides

through Japanese landscapes
each believing in Spring
because of the absence
as when a container

is emptied & illuminates
the darkness.   The idea
remains the same   supported
inside the target when leaving the string

for what we are seeing
are not the disguised
defined forever in solitary moments
but what we shall be if we keep on living –

twisted mosaics of wisteria
waiting for the past to start
upon the luxurious border
of this stunning isolation.